APOCALYPTIC NARRATIVE AND OTHER POEMS

POETRY BY
RODNEY JONES

The Story They Told Us of Light · 1980
The Unborn · 1985
Transparent Gestures · 1989
Apocalyptic Narrative and Other Poems · 1993

APOCALYPTIC
NARRATIVE

AND OTHER POEMS

RODNEY JONES

HOUGHTON MIFFLIN COMPANY

BOSTON   NEW YORK   1993

For information about permission to reproduce selections
from this book, write to Permissions, Houghton Mifflin Company,
215 Park Avenue South, New York, New York 10003.

Library of Congress Cataloging-in-Publication Data

Jones, Rodney, date.
Apocalyptic narrative and other poems / Rodney Jones.
p.   cm.
ISBN 0-395-67526-X
I. Title.
PS3560.05263A86   1993
811'.54—dc20   93-15771
            CIP

Printed in the United States of America

BP 10 9 8 7 6 5 4 3 2 1

Book design by Melodie Wertelet

Acknowledgments and credits appear on page 70.

For Gloria, Alexis, and Samuel
and in memory of Everette Maddox

CONTENTS

APOCALYPTIC NARRATIVE AND OTHER POEMS

So quickly I forgot the things that brought me joy,
The way a blind man assumes the obvious dark
Of a familiar room, atlas of rug and banister,

The depths of stairs, the torque of glass knobs,
The durable links compounding out of ease,
So many strong and nurturing people that I loved

Dimmed among habits. I could see so clearly
Each scene of injury, places where known tempers
Flared and defiled, even the mentioned things

That never happened, the cycles of dogma and ultimatums,
The married woman's secret upstart mind, and all
Of those who were like priests, in their celibate duties,

Like a field mouse wintering between the studs,
Like something thought of so long before it was written
That part of its body had fallen away—which is why

I woke at 3 A.M., festering some old rage at words,
But stood back, knowing the animal poised there
At the center of life, and, sealed inside of me,

The world's unvarying tracks, all marks of shyness
That follow the natural shyness of the child,
The time of one man and one woman in youth,

And the drier kisses, the tongue receding in the jaw,
Not the song, but the humming after the song,
The barrier, the quiet knowledge, called for and unspoken.

Willie Cooper, what are you doing here, this early in your death?

To show us what we are, who live by twisting words—
Heaven is finished. A poet is as anachronistic as a blacksmith.

You planted a long row and followed it. Signed your name X
        for seventy years.
Poverty is not hell. Fingers cracked by frost
And lacerated by Johnson grass are not hell.

Hell is what others think we are.

You told me once, "Never worry."
Your share of worry was as small as your share of the profits,

Mornings-after of lightning and radiator shine,
The beater Dodge you bought in late October—
By February, its engine would hang from a rafter like a ham.

You had a free place to stay, a wife
Who bore you fourteen children. Nine live still.

You live in the stripped skeleton of a shovelbill cat.

Up here in the unforgivable amnesia of libraries,
Where many poems lie dying of first-person omniscience,
The footnotes are doing their effete dance, as always.

But only one of your grandsons will sleep tonight in Kilby Prison.
The hackberry in the sand field will be there long objectifying.

Once I was embarrassed to have to read for you
A letter from Shields, your brother in Detroit,
A hick-grammared, epic lie of northern women and money.

All I want is to get one grain of the dust to remember.

I think it was your advice I followed across the oceans.
What can I do for you now?

These fulsome nouns, these abbreviations of the air,
Are not real, but two of them may fit a small man
I knew in high school, who, seeing an accident,
Stopped one day, leapt over a mangled guardrail,
Took a mother and two children from a flooded creek,
And lifted them back to the world. In the dark,
I do not know, there is no saying, but he pulled
Them each up a tree, which was not the tree of life
But a stooped Alabama willow, flew three times
From the edge of that narrow bridge as though
From the selfless shore of a miracle, and came back
To the false name of a real man, Arthur Peavahouse.
He could sink a set shot from thirty feet. One night
I watched him field a punt and scat behind a wall
Of blockers like a butterfly hovering an outhouse.
He did not love the crashing of bodies. He
Did not know that mother and her three children
But went down one huge breath to their darkness.
There is no name for that place, you cannot
Find them following a white chain of bubbles
Down the muddy water of these words. But I saw
Where the rail sheared from the bridge—which is
Not real since it was replaced by a wider bridge.
Arthur Peavahouse weighed a hundred and twenty pounds.
Because he ran well in the broken field, men
Said he was afraid. I remember him best
At a laboratory table, holding a test tube
Up to the light, arranging equations like facts,
But the school is air over a parking lot. You
Are too far from that valley for it to come
All the way true, although it is not real.
Not two miles from that bridge, one afternoon
In March, in 1967, one of my great-uncles,
Clyde Maples, a farmer and a Commissioner of Roads,
And his neighbor, whose name I have forgotten,

Pulled more than a hundred crappies off three
Stickups in that creek—though the creek is not
Real and the valley is a valley of words. You
Would need Clyde Maples to find Arthur Peavahouse,
And you would need Clyde Maples' side yard
Of roadgraders and bulldozers to get even part
Of Clyde Maples, need him like the crappies
Needed those stickups in the creek to tell them
Where they were. Every spring that creek
Darkens with the runoff of hog-lots and barns,
Spreading sloughs, obscuring sorghum and corn.
On blind backwater full schoolbuses roll
Down buried roads. Arthur Peavahouse was smart
To run from the huge tackles and unthinking
To throw himself into that roiling water
And test the reality of his arms and his lungs.
Many times I have thought everything I have said
Or thought was a lie, moving some blame or credit
By changing a name, even the color of a lip or bush,
But whenever I think of the lie that stands for truth,
I think of Arthur Peavahouse, and not his good name,
But him deciding, as that car settled to the bottom,
To break free and live for at least one more moment
Upward toward light and the country of words
While the other child, the one he could not save,
Shrugged behind him in the unbreakable harness.

The guns and the young soldiers on the road did not terrify me,
That clear and luminous December afternoon,
Dragging the sailboat down the lawn to the edge of the lake,
But, in the shallows, the water
Was strung with the living coil and snare of *lama*.

We had to wait, and the father and the little girl
Working with machete and net
Entered the mind for a little while,

Pulled back the veil of concatenating words, the odd thousands of books,
The twenty years jabbering in schools,
The months as a copywriter, the months in the warehouse,
The summers in the tubing factory, and the summers in the ditch,
The years stumbling after balls, the years listening
After inscrutable numbers and dates and grammars:

I stood in the cotton field. I was just her age.
In my mind, it was autumn. The boysenberries were ripe,
But I did not pick them. I bent
To the searing rag- and sheet-bearing bolls and I did
What others did. I grew up,

Let the scenes fall on top of each other,
Looked down through the skylines, faces, mountains, and coasts,
And then
Witnessed the ibis,
Byzantine among the eucalyptus,
Heard the freckled symmetry in the black bathing suit
Extol the virtues of Sai Baba and Silva Mind Control

While the father went down with his machete,
Gathered in his arms a dark, ribbony clot
Of the dirty green carpet of *lama*,
And brought it up to his daughter.

She took it, one strand at a time, and placed it in the net
With such a languorous ostentation and craft
It was like the first sentence from "Sunday Morning"
Or it was like the sentence Ortega meant to make
When he wrote that we are all lost
And mainly liars.

So the present lingered there for a long time
Cutting a clean swath through the *lama*
So we could sail out toward that island
Where once we had made love
Under three circling Piper Cubs
And a camouflage helicopter left over from Vietnam.

Behind us, stolid as Job, lovelier than Montana,
The rivulets of the sleeping volcanoes
Hung like the pleats of drawn curtains.

I suppose that just behind there, behind the coffee,
Bitter and innocent children were hurting each other
With all manner of weaponry,
On hundreds of channels and in thousands of periodicals.

The week before, no more than thirty kilometers to the southeast,
Drunk *guerilleros* or government soldiers
Drove out into a pasture with bazookas
And took out twenty-one imperialist or insurrectionist cows,

Depending on which reports one believed.

You think it easy to know the truth of a country,
But there was only one instant the father and his daughter
Slipped back up into the trees and became the shade

I would remember more than the water
At the party the following night, before the solid thunk of the explosive,
When I turned and found a third of the city dark.

Holiest of American cities, sublime hostess,
Conductor of the nightmare chase,
The miraculous escape, the midnight
Lightning seduction, this is my movie,

Adolescent, erotic, requiring darkness,
In which a boy goes like a ship probing
The cosmologies of the décolletage,
And still I feel the guidance of your saints:

Clara Bow, that bird peeping up from a dim cleft;
Lillian Gish, the almost transparent; Mae West,
That cloud that precipitates before our eyes.
Flirtations that led to our being.

Fantasia of the scholar and the masturbator.
I have to close my eyes to see Rita Hayworth
In *Gilda*, in that scene where she glides
Down into the casino, the hair a dull flame,

The skin of an undiluted and primeval whiteness.
I have no idea which chord she struck
That her beauty slips from me like a fish.
Tall and lean, she will forget everything.

But I remember my own girl, black Irish,
Saturdays flashing hot on the cool vinyl seats
Under the drive-in's stars. Serene moods
Decompressing into laughter Sunday nights,

Owl-hooting when we parked before church.
Small, difficult breasts. Then the sermon,
I half remember, on the evils of Hollywood—
Temptations of money, temptations of the flesh.

April in the woods, beatitudes of the thighs,
And when she broke it off, she turned so meek
And easily hurt, I mistook guilt for logic.
I wanted to go on worshipping the world.

Holiest of American cities, men with torches
Run through your streets. The old scenes burn.
Stupid factory of immaculate craftsmen,
Tooling into dreams the beautiful human ore,

A smoke goes up. Eros and erosion.
The teenage gods of violence and sensuality.
The face of Winger. The face of Streep.
Not much happens on nights in the Midwest,

But pick a story, any story, and put it there.
We know other dreams than love.
We know one beauty and it redeems
Everything as tragedy when it is taken away.

The poor people in Springfield go to Dayton to be miserable
    in style.
They can hug themselves when they lie side by side on the
    iron cots.
They can luxuriate in one red bean held under the tongue.
For them, a discarded refrigerator crate, tipped on its side
    and lined with plastic bags,
Is the green shore of an island and a palace's velvet halls.
Every morning they check out of the Club St. Vincent de Paul,
And they clump in the warm gusts that scowl up from the sewers.

They can strip the aluminum from gutters as their mothers
    harvested eggs from boxes of straw.
Against that snow that is all edge, they can wobble and careen
    from bumper to lightpole,
Dancing with the parking meter before dying into the hydrant
    under the fire escape.
Deliriously happy, they lift the sweetest and heaviest wine
    and sink down where the metal is warm,
Across from the cafeteria and that other richest trough,
Kingdom of heaven on earth, emerald dumpster of the pizzeria.

What does it matter if I heap treasure from the stick people,
    far off and helpless, fluttering of brown coats?
Their lives are not my life. I come as a tourist to their woe.
But I remember how quickly dark fell, twenty years ago, thumbing
    from Greensboro to Boulder.
I carried one change of clothes, a notebook, and a little more
    than seven dollars,
And I thought I could live by the grace of hippies and priests
    or, failing that,
Prey on park squirrels and the ducks from municipal ponds.

I did not have to go that way. I could have gone on wrestling
     those big sacks of fertilizer
From the co-op's storage bins to the beds of pickup trucks,
Or bludgeoning ice from the front steps of the coliseum,
But I had to get it straight from the black road and the mouth
     of the blue norther.
There is a high ledge under every overpass where you can sleep
     if it is not too cold.
One morning I woke there beside a short man, a carnie and ex-con
     reared
In the Tennessee Industrial School and a dozen foster homes.

We talked a stupid dream of burglary. We committed the crime
     of brotherhood.
Then, hungry and stiff, we trudged up the ramp to a truckstop,
     where he meant
To convince me to knife a man for three hundred dollars
     locked in a drawer.
He said we could get away, we could take any one of those semis
     idling outside that place
Like great buffaloes blowing clouds and clearing their throats.
But I have taken nothing. I have gotten away clean to Illinois.

Tonight the steaks frown up at me through the odor of blood,
And the poor need no help from poems to limp down the alley
     and up into the van.
They glide to Dayton. They check in to the Club St. Vincent de Paul.
Whatever it is, it is not much that makes a man more
     than a scrap of paper
Torn out of a notebook and thrown from the window of a bus,
     but it is more than nothing.
If he holds himself straight up and does not take the life
Next to his own, give him that much. Leave him to his joy.

Far off and horrible. I hope it is not true.
But the Japanese knew a little English.
One of them would get you by your name,
Call you into the jungle, and slit your throat.

Hunched there each morning for two weeks
Of 1944. Heard, over the riot
Of his own heart, the syllables of the roll,
And sang a live man to the knife.

I was told this by my father,
Who heard it from Cleveland Wilheit,
Who was there at Corregidor or Guadalcanal.
It is not much. It is only one whisper

In a gallery of whispers, but you have
To take somebody's word for the world.
Must strain small truths from large
To wake that one man alive. He does not

Know you but trembles and calls your name.
One night two of my countrymen
Lay for him in the bushes. Before light,
They took the red sin of the tongue.

They peeled the skin from each arm
And nailed a man-message to a palm.
You are supposed to believe your own name.
You are supposed to believe the good Christ

Forgives everything unmentionable forever,
But they handed him one ear and one eye.
Almost fifty years ago they left him
Suffering and alive, student of language.

Down there in the barrio, wallow of pigs and runty dogs, he grasps
    the cold night by the throat,
And he shakes it like a bad fig or a rat.
He lifts it out of the grunting-in-place and the scuffling to gather sticks
    for the fire,
And he sends it up through the miffs and the hangovers,
Over the razory wire of the stucco walls and the turrets of sleeping guards,
    so I must hear it
High in my room in Escalón, and so wake in the clear man-anger
    of predawn,
Though I do not know what it is saying, that six-pound switch on the sun,
    that ore of dumplings and casseroles,
But also now the cars grumbling off curbs and out of garages
    are joining in,
And brother cries rear from a hundred roofs held down by
    coconuts and stones,
And, from deep in the years, the evangelist Purnell Hughes crows
    his forty-two dollars of hellfire and brimstone,
And would-be governors and lovers woo from beer joints and boardrooms.

So I must hear it all, as I have heard myself, as I have heard every man
    stretching by the skin of his own voice
To say some secret, unspeakable thing, and dawn comes to Escalón.
The long war of the night has left its clandestine tracks, its motley
    of privilege and scars.
The amputee tips from his mat and clambers onto his rickety crutches,
    the offices that sell Japanese typewriters
And the offices that sell Korean automobiles roll back their bars,
    silence in the *casa presidencial*,
And now the first reluctant crowds drift down from the white houses
    with red tile roofs
And, from farther off, along the green arroyos that crimp the cone
    of the volcano,
Each mud and cardboard hut struts the black plumage of its fire.
The soldiers are walking their rifles like dogs, and now and then a bomb
    shatters a pole,
And still the rooster swells and drives his six red syllables like a spike.

It is a small sermon or speech I might have made, but did not, for how
    could a man puff himself up,
Throw his voice from the rightness of love, and not tear a rift in paradise?
What difference would it make? High or low, pig-grunt, dog-howl, bomb-
    blast, mantra, and benediction?
For as long as I can remember, I have known or heard of one or another
    of that low breed of saints who mean
To concentrate millennia in a sound or stop the human heart
    with a thought.
My love, my circle of gifts, I have said a few things all right, my least
    will, my frail
Claims staked like the rooster's ever-repeating irrevocable deed
    on the air.
When I was a boy, I meant to be good and quiet, to own nothing
    and no one, but now
It seems I must take my cue from the night's blind tripe and the shill
    of the morning sun,
To call what is mine up from the depths or make biscuits of these words.

WHITE MEXICANS

In Central America in the fifties
They had two words for people from the South.
My father-in-law told me
Early one morning while we were eating
Eggs and bacon beside the Pacific Ocean,
And I was astonished and amazed
To find that we were not seen everywhere
As the genteel daughters
And sons of the one living God.
I thought that we were, the earth over,
Three peoples: black, white, and trash.
In North Alabama in the fifties,
The Mexicans did not stray far
From the truck patches, the Jews stayed
In the Old Testament, but there were
Germans in the next town, Cullman,
And a woman who had lost an arm
Playing with an explosive doll
Made by one of the loyalists
To the old country in World War One.

One morning at the country store
Where the men used to go to trade
Heart-rending jokes and legends
Of frontier murders and bluetick hounds
For Pyrrhic credit on a lunch
Of Vienna Sausages, stale crackers,
And a lukewarm bottle of Ma Cherie,
I heard the storekeeper,
Henry Hardin, whisper "Dago,"
A word that I had never heard
And had no use for, to describe
The mustache of a salesman,
Who had, after elucidating the praises
Of a miraculous new chocolate bar,
Said that he had once played

For the Senators but lived now
Just east of Macon, Georgia.
Everything that Henry Hardin sold,
Rat poison or bread, is dirt.

The country store is grass.
The old seeds who ran the General Merchandises
In Georgia, Mississippi, and Alabama
Have crossed the Jordan River
And ascended into Abraham's bosom
Or risked the Stygian straits
And descended into the pits
To trade with the big boys.
And the athletic salesman,
If he is still alive, rushes
From convention to convention,
Singing a new computer game
Manufactured outside Los Angeles
By a handful of patriots
Still loyal to Nguyen Van Thieu.

My dark plum, my white Mexican,
German, Welsh, and Mayan son,
I did not have to be born in that place.
I could have chosen to live in a world
Where all the races come together
And refer to each other cautiously
In great universities.
I could have said
One herd is gathering underground.
It is not much. It stinks
To heaven. Like the place
Where I was born, it relives
Its defeat by forgetting its evils.
Like marriage, it wants
To simplify love by narrowing
The field.

Yet once when the cotton
Was all picked, the hay
Was in, and the cornstalks
Were stripped to stobs,
We gathered in one church,
Black, white, and trash,
Because that good carpenter,
Oliver Hodge, had died
Broke and without family,
And so we sat there fidgeting
Through six horrible hymns,
Four prayers, and a eulogy
Cribbed from a book
And preached by a total stranger,
Then, gently, gently
Bearing the casket uphill
To the grave a few strong
Neighbors had freely dug,
Surely in that instant,
If we lowered our heads
And did not speak too loudly,
We were loyal to paradise.

Seeing how almost everyone who has known and loved me believes
    in the eternal life and the immortal soul,
How do I tell them it does not work for me up there on high
    where the prayers light
In the balmy rafters of Zion and the eminent ether of Christ?

They would say my brain has been washed clean by the professors
    of philosophy and science.
They would say I have forgotten the river behind the old church
    where, when I was baptized,
My grandmother witnessed the burden lifted and the body made new.

Already, they know, if one of them asks a blessing, my eyes fly open.
    The afterlife glares up from the table.
Here are the molecules of a seventeenth-century smile.
    It will go as it has gone before.
The gastrin and hydrochloric acid will play their duet on the lasagna.

I could say, at least, a slow tree is faster than a man. That appetite
    endears us to this life.
But still they'd watch that recent spirit rise above that certain chair.
    Sixty years he followed
A team of Belgian horses and dreamed of writing a great gospel song.

It would be better not to bring up the crafting of the pearly gates
    and the paving of the streets of gold.
It would hurt them if I showed them how each angel was plaited
    from a dead girl and a living bird.
They would ask themselves, how can a man live with so little hope?

And just as well I swallow words I might have said along with bread
    if all my reservations
In the end amount to snubs that make the dead and living fools.
    I know, if I said something, they would not get mad.
They would look at each other with that fierce glow of forgiveness.

Then they would pass me the preserves and bring a cup of coffee,
    black and sugarless.
They would frown as they saw me falling, with no net or rope,
    past the uncharmed stars,
And they would pray for me. They would hate to see me burn.

How slowly I came away from that vision of death
As a stage and stood before the butcher case,
Confessional of the cynics, pickled pig's feet,
Shining chops, insensitive to transcendence.
I had not seen the eyes of the lamb when I took
The white gristle in one paw, and I had not
Heard the lowing of the calves when I let
The grease drift down my chin and my arms.
The colors must have moved me more than the taste.
The reds at the hams and the shoulders
Might have been bars lit for the night.
I took them in my mouth and I left them ash.
I loved the roasts and in particular I loved
The duck, the veal, and the filet mignon
Before the cardiologists left me weeds and fish.
Only then I gave in a little to guilt.
Only then I began to look east for wisdom,
But not until Everette Maddox died
Did I begin to believe in reincarnation.
The dance he had done on tables made
Me look for him in the cat, and the way
He had curled up drunk pointed to the dog.
His brain was his glory. I did not like it
How he set a feast in his liver and his heart.
Those last months he slept in a dump truck.
He scribbled constantly in the Maple Leaf
And at Carrollton Station. I hated it
How he suffered so proudly and inconsolably.
In the letters, especially, you can see the scope.
He carried the nineteenth century with him.
He moved like a bird between Twain and Keats.
But it was not the brain and it was not the meat.
Not until I got my knife under the seal
Of the plastic urn and ran my fingers
Through the grit and the splinters of bone

Did I begin to believe the soul meant other
Than ancient desperation and lonely desire,
And not until we marched through the streets
Did I begin to look into the eyes of men
With something other than courtesy and fear.
Bob Woolf glided in his dark suit. Sam
Maisel fidgeted. There were four hundred.
Fred Kasten had the ashes just behind the band.
I could see Boswell, Schilling, and Smith,
And the rest of life, dripping from hooks,
Jerusalem of lamb or Mecca of beef,
But just that once I saw the heavens open
And heard the soul shrieking as it entered the tree.
For just that minute I was out of my mind with grief.

Are the replacements in? Dove-colored britches, black shirts,
    harbingers of the look
That already brushed past me as I entered by the east gate,
    like a noun searching for a verb,
And walked slowly under the names of unimaginable families,
    past shops where the same immaculate
Fishnet kept sprawling across driftwood sequined with shells,
And the manikins went on working out the problems of the world.

One of the manikins had frosted hair and wore braces,
    another, her goldleaf dreadlocks
Skimming the pages of *War and Peace*, exotic tableaus
    of the Scandinavian and Japanese,
Ambassadorial saints of some mythical cultural commonwealth
    that speaks in a British accent
In the United States and talks, on PBS, compulsively,
Of the great heroes and heroines of opera and classical music.

But mainly it's California the windows send, in surfboards
    and dark glasses,
In bikinis strung a season away, in greed's modest future.
On Friday night, you would think the world empties there
    and tumbles in a bee-mill
Of inverted weariness and lust, though it is possible,
    just past the Vision Center,
To look straight ahead and greet no one, to move quietly.

And if you stopped as I stopped outside the tuxedo rental,
    in that space
That is always empty, in that place that is not a place,
    but domed, vaulted, and fountained,
If you walked there, with death still fresh in your thoughts
As a bone-needle driven under one nail from the ashes,
And smelled the sweat of the cloggers and the Elvis imitators,

And felt the live swamp dried and buckled beneath you,
And hesitated by Sears and The Locker and Pier One,
You would want all grief to end there.
You would remember the fraud of the chateau and the lie
    of the cathedral.
You would want great shoes to replace the eyes and beard.

You would want the clove cigarettes and wicker elephants
    to restore the fingers.
You would want a linen suit to stand for the legs and arms.
You would have that mutable god, that prayer to things,
And that religion, whose prophets are actors and salesmen,
    whose scripture is television,
Whose temples bulge with icons disposable as sacrifice.

There was a cardboard woman outside the jewelry store.
Where there had been pain, there was a Japanese car.
Where there was a voice, whole orchestras were shrunken
    onto disks.
This was where the corridor lapsed down the long banister.
This is what I came to shining in the depths.

That mirror-shard, that glittering grist at the heart.
And then the lot, identical forgetfulness and distraction,
The gray sins, the white depressions and red divorces
    parked side by side,
The rusty gains, the late-model losses, everything
    waiting to move us again,
To ease us back into the traffic with our gifts.

1.

Clearing the boxes, tins of stale biscuits, powdered eggs
And milk, dried soybeans, we found our last provisions
Whole except for syringes and numbing drugs
Imaginative junkies had stripped from the medical kits.
The water was still pure in each forty-gallon jug,
The U.S. Government cheese barely rinded with mold.
Two weeks' rations for ten thousand, the foreman said.
One man hummed. Another told a joke of diddling
A woman so fat he didn't know if it was out or in,
Though none brooked the hotter subject underneath:
The exponential x-ray that would blast all buildings,
Bridges, and trees, or the fine ash, fallen in dreams,
The fever and vomiting, the putrefaction of the skin—
That blind nightmare we fattened for forty years.
It ran with hell. It ended. It was not the world
We took on wobbling dollies, up the steep ledge
Under the bat-fouled bluff, and dumped in the truck,
But strangely disappointing, then, to see the cave
Emptied to darkness and know, too, the whole place
Would go to spiders, the entrance be boarded up,
Though, later, a local dentist established there
A live nativity so popular the church put bleachers up,
And once the fundamentalist governor came and stood
Before us playing a simple shepherd with a crook,
Commemorating hope. The mountain overhead, five
Hundred million tons of limestone, was not enough.

2.

Too much of the trappings of our imagined ends
Depends on the hoax and rot of lapsed mythologies,
Horned broodstock of the dreamlife, ghosts
Of some earlier holiness, wisdomed up from warnings
And grafted onto laws already weighted down
With ancient torts, preferments, property rights—
But the dream believes most what logic denies:
Those crusty gods, those fires that gut the heart.
When I was a boy in Alabama, I loved my mother's
Biscuits, March rain pelleting on the tin roof,
My crippled, one-eyed dog; but feared the dark,
The snaky pond, the neighbor kid who'd come
On stormy nights and hunker just beyond the porch
Chronicling missiles and megatons, the joy
In his voice as he whispered, V*aporized, vaporized*,
And more than him, the six-foot-six evangelist,
Last night of the revival, Bible wriggling high
On one blue palm as he rhapsodized on Armageddon.
I thought, *Christ eats the dead.* And think now
How the planet would turn as well without us,
As when a finger is lifted from a glass
And the water regains its shape, or sometimes,
Of a sudden, one night of childhood will clear
Above the general mist: a rock, a teardrop cedar—
We stand there linking hands before the fire,
Sing low, demand to hear the ghost story again,
Complain incessantly it is too mild unless
Blood drips from the banister and the headless
Woman shrieks and writhes up out of the fire.
We are not thrilled unless we are terrified.

3

Only in the tamed trembling of a poem, I had believed
Some kindness might survive, and "Cool your jets,"
He told me when I chided him for barging in late
And slamming down his books as I gravely read
Gray's "Elegy," a thing I shouldn't remember
Except it had a point. "Hey man, cool your jets!"
One of the teenage wisdoms: Beauty is final,
Devastating, absolute. In ugliness, there is hope,
In trashed rivers, in the slightly obese girl
Who sat beside me twenty-five years ago as the bus
Groaned toward evil Tuscaloosa. And so I came
Like Amos to the black-light, pop-poster salons,
Read Vonnegut, heard the Dead, dropped mescaline
In numb, freaked-out America, that year of Tet,
Said, "I won't go. I won't kiss the ass of death"—
But lacked the ossifying cool, the Stratocaster,
Ponytail, and rap that arched the backs of girls,
And so dug the French thing from Michaud to Villon
And languished in the rigor mortis of the *I Ching*.
And when Frog McEntire, God's aboriginal hippie, dressed me
For the drag ball—black midi and cultured pearls,
Matching bag, a platinum wig from the Dollar Store—
And squired me across the yard, a skeleton
Stooped and shat in a can. Four bikers roared
Up on hogs. He said, "Man, it's happening, and
I can't fucking believe it." He said, "Too much."
A bamboo screen, white kitchen, Jim-Ella's crowd
Raising blond dollops of hash on glowing spoons,
Gay, petulant, bouffant as Medusa's beauty shop—
And down the candled hall, black-jacketed Warhol,
Albino and amphetamined, beside his latest star.

4.

This is the world sex saved us from: not fame
But indifference, not the moment of adulation
But the crowd dispersing through the alleys
Near the stadium, one season with its star
Dimming in empathetic roles, the nurse,
The guidance counselor, the sage of Mini-Pads,
Ascending the channels, eternities of Prague and Omaha.
In Carbondale, it comes in snowy, cracked, oblique.
"It's something in the water," a woman told me,
But the party soaked its last liqueurs. Jokes sobered.
A physicist spoke of a new calendar he'd devised,
Beginning after television, after the bomb. "We are,"
He said, "so terribly junior to that God."
When I was a boy, I loved my mother's biscuits
And feared the dark; deep space; vengeance
Of the desert prophets driving their vision dogs
Until the sexual animal was treed in fire.
"It's better," she said, pulling on lace panties
Behind the church, "when you believe in hell."
But it does no good to rub the times together,
Gabbling on that old string because we are strangers
In the peace that intervenes between lovemakings.
Or to see it all in an erupting instant given out
As when the artsies stroll all in black they know
It will fly apart, glass city, omnipotent, vulnerable.
And "God is orgasm," she whispered years ago
And lay back, small and white, on the dark rug.
It is not enough. It bores us and it only works
As an ending once unless we come to it without will,
And we come, stupid and crazy, believing in love,
And go winding back down the temple's easy stairs,
Near sleep, plummet past the owl and the mole,
And Twain wrote of ringworm as divine intervention.

5.

After a while it occurs to us and at the simplest times
When the lights go suddenly out and we fumble
Lampward through the deep clutter of the rooms,
The past is mainly dark, but not what we thought,
Squirreled away in a box, all its books shut,
Its songs and anecdotes previews of oblivion.
It will happen again, the terrifying sex, the light
Flesh makes blazing quietly underground,
Hendrix and Joplin, Morrison and Allman;
Talmadge, my childhood friend, Patrick's lover,
Who sang beautifully "How Great Thou Art"
And stewarded on the Chicago–London route,
Before expiring, according to the local daily,
"From ambiguous complications of pneumonia";
Silly flowers on the ridge at Grayson Highlands,
Foxglove and wood sorrel, blueprints of mania
Where we sat and heard the charismatics testify:
And when God called me to his service, I got
My hammer and saw, put the ladder in the truck
And drove to Mexico. And built His holy church.
Fog was lifting. Earlier rain had passed
East, whirled up the Holston watershed,
And now, as the light of the world came skipping
And dappling vague rosettes among the stones,
A man rose from the lee of the highest boulder
And spoke: *Brothers and sisters, strength*
Is not enough. I ate steroids like candy,
Bulked up and benched five hundred pounds,
But it was emptiness until I accepted grace
And gave it up. The money, the cars, the girls.
And now, pump iron for Him, praise His name—
Listen, only a thin layer of skin
Keeps us from squirting into the world.

6.

This is the last testimony of the last days, made
On Sunday as cars rattle over the iron bridge
And on down Chautauqua, a stone and glass chapel
Founded on tax shelters, a modest Episcopalian miracle.
Light of the world, this is the joke love makes.
I was saved in Alabama and backslid to some good
Loving early in the colicky infancy of the bomb.
I hope my son won't run with zombies to the end.
The deal I'd rather make with the dead is fun,
The victories of peace: clean pillows, luxuries
Of orange juice and toast, which need no blessing,
Because the god sleeps, and nothing worships us.
No prophet rivets us to dread. No demon comes
On the tails of black jets, only iced tea and soup,
The Cowboys and the Bears, the endless human hope
That, backed up to the goal, insists that this
Is all there will be. This is all there will ever be;
But if you should read this, far off in the future,
Small and indefatigable dots, still holding on,
Still balancing on a blind tentacle of science,
Praise us that once we lay down without prevention
And started it, whatever it is salted in the genes,
Recessive trump that, of its own passiveness, waits
Through the unplayable hand and survives exactness.
Praise our uplifted thighs and the cries we made
As the seed harvest bared the singing nerve. Praise
Our electrons humming down cables from the split atom.
Praise the Beatles, W. C. Fields, and Bessie Smith.
Praise our many knowledges that came from accidents.
From our six fingers come your corrugating fins.
From our eyes come the balls of your reticulate feet.
From our brains your batteries. From our livers
Your encyclotropic perfumes. And if it is genesis
You would study, imagine us. We lived here.
We made our choice between the virus and the germ.

More than once, the brain dies here, dies on the name
Of a cloud or flower, and the watch is flushed down the toilet;
Marriages are passed from one to another
Like buckets of water at an old-time fire.
And still each spring the premonition bird
Feathers the same nest in the groin.
And still the addresses and the phone numbers fly apart.
The news, with its joyless victims, does not save us.
Love is all becalmed or starts too fitfully
As though God and the stupid heart conspired
To checker each breakfast table with silence,
And often in the early light it is easy to believe
That face that shines forever and never ages,
But the ocean and the trees come to us at night,
And sometimes we look at each other as the ocean
And trees are seen from the comfort of a window,
Behind which all the points have been won or lost
And history shrugs its indifferent shoulders
And walks across the carpet from its bath
Humming the forgetfulness of a popular song,
A song of victims, a song of late courage
We meant to honor once with money and applause.
O surely if there were some cause, we would think
To organize communication, transportation, the shipments
Of shelter and food, or go there ourselves
To be martyrs if there were a new Auschwitz to die in.

AT SUMMERFORD'S NURSING HOME

Like plants in pots, they sit along the wall,
Breached at odd angles, wheelchairs locked,
Or drift in tortoise-calm ahead of doting sons:

Some are still continent and wink at others
Who seem to float in and out of being here,
And one has balked beside the check-in desk—

A jaunty shred of carrot glowing on one lip,
He fumbles a scared hug from each little girl
Among the carolers from the Methodist Church

Until two nurses shush him and move him on.
There is a snatch of sermon from the lounge,
And then my fourth-grade teacher washes up,

And someone else—who is it?—nodding the pale
Varicose bloom of his skull: the bald postman,
The butcher from our single grocery store?

Or is that me, graft on another forty years?
Will I become that lump, attached to tubes
That pump in mush and drain the family money?

Or will I be the one who stops it with a gun,
Or, more insensibly, with pills and alcohol?
And would it be so wrong to liberate this one

Who stretches toward me from his bed and moans
Above the constant chlorine of cleaning up
When from further down the hall I hear the first

Transmogrifying groans: the bestial O and O
Repeating like a mantra that travels long
Roads of nerves to move a sound that comes

And comes but won't come finally up to words,
Not the oldest ones that made the stories go,
Not even *love*, or *help*, or *hurt*, but goodbye

And hello, grandfather, the rest of your life
Coiled around you like a rope, while one by
One, we strange relatives lean to be recognized.

ON THE ELEVENTH ANNIVERSARY OF DIVORCE

Surely that man is dead, who tiptoed in the kitchen door,
And that woman sleeps, or is it memory that closes
Her off alone with a natural history or book of dreams
While he crosses the floor quietly, though there is no
Longer any need to speak of difference or even to recall
How opposition fashioned and drew them into one bond.
Set against napalm, chauvinism, and the Puritan church,
That life is over, the foolish, childish, faithful one,
Gone to soiled laundry and dishes glaring in the sink,
Or both already are dying here, as she begins again
To try to say the hard wound that would put it right
And he leaks from each confrontation like a sieve.
But fix them earlier in the grave of that buried year
As they walk the sandstone bluff upriver to the cave,
Both shirtless, the red braids falling to their waists
As in a famous bad movie that he is gladly acting out
While she flails at gnats and nettles with her wrist
And maybe almost says the secret she will never say,
Though now he only stops it with a kiss that blends
Back into the day of minor troubles and vantage points
Like a skink on a rock or a bird they can't identify.
And then the birds go silent. Both will remember that
Years later, when they touch, and it is often difficult
To urge the body to that blindness of circumstance,
That fish-gullible stare beyond the out-of-date
And merely friendly, when, in that swim toward the future,
They strain together and the thing begins in its ending
Up from the grand sump and swallowing nerve of the hips,
And, back in their minds, they are torn gently forward,
As page after page is sundered from the calendar
Until the trial and conviction of beauty demand
That they become us, who lasted longer than many wars.

FAILED MEMORY EXERCISE

The water tank above the trees, and then the town,
Lord God, the sudden, blunt, exhilarating shock
Of pavement against the chert of the bottom road,

Bare schoolyard, white clinic, a block of stores
Like a test for names, beginning with the P.O.,
By which, in late autumn, the loaded wagons came,

The colts wheeling behind the great sober mares,
And turned east, clattering toward the cotton gin,
And returned empty, and faded beyond the tracks,

Beyond those yards, where one day the sallow
Dozers rolled and skinned back the flowerbeds
For the pumps and grease rack of the new Shell;

But begin again, for the dark green Lincoln rises
To its lube and crests where Zetty's kitchen was:
The black gush withers and dribbles to a drip,

And memory gums like shavings in the burnt oil
Now that plywood masks the windows of the stores,
Which test me as I bump awake above the Atlantic

Or wait in the plant-hung lobby of a hotel
In Atlanta or Montreal and answer then, though
I do not know the nature of the questions, true

Or false, fill-in-the-blanks south from the P.O.:
Three grocers, Leona Patterson's Fabric Box,
The shuttered bank, the poolhall din and smoke,

And this would have been a Saturday, *Sabrina*
Playing at the Cameo, the farmers scooping
Sweet feed and calf manna from the silvery bins

Of H. R. Summerford and Sons, General Merchandise,
But stop now, for I see the man without a nose
Like a pencil point ground to a nub and breaking

There against the efflorescence of the barbershop,
And stare again into that hole beneath the eyes
Where I must have thought I'd spy the brain itself

Before my gaze dropped to seize on missing tiles,
A blond curl, a plate engraved ACME MFG., INC. —
Those things that wore away and primed a vacancy.

But he sat there while my distant cousin shined his shoes,
And then he simply walked across Main to the depot,
A place I can't forget, since its beams were ripped out,

Numbered, and shipped east to some resurrection bistro
Where one can cop a decent blintz and espresso now
That the trains don't stop and no one's keeping store.

How did I miss this isthmus of old bricks between the Shelter Workshop
    and the Dominion Bank,
This bumpy lane, not even a street now, but pot-holed and tar-streaked
    and smeared with the indiscriminate droppings of pigeons?
In the seventies, these were the blocks I loved, squat little downtown,
    its Roxy closed
And boarded up, the domed theater dark and mattress-strewn,
    a few drunks sleeping it off there
In the place of dreams, with the spidery stars of a faded velvet heaven
    falling into their beards.
I stood outside that place one afternoon, vagrant beneath the random
    lettering of the broken marquee.
I was not in that much trouble. Why did I turn then and look so closely?

Except for the first mountains to the east, which, in March, were still
    purple-brown and crested with snow,
Everything was used up, rusted or sere, warped on winter's flinty edge—
    just left there—
Buildings and men, and I loved them for their cracked faces and greasy food.
I took each rip and splinter as Baudelaire took his cripples and imbeciles,
As the true pessimist relishes the catastrophe that confirms his faith.
Let Baptists roll in mountain rivers, shouting hosannas to their holy ghost.
    More than the mountains,
I loved that majorette in pink cowgirl fringe as she sank with her 1940s
    cola into the acid of the concrete wall behind the hardware.
And more than any flower or shrub, I loved that slattern of a broken hotel
Where Jimmie Rodgers once sang of his own loneliness and bitter trains.

It took him years. By the time he found his songs, he was dying in public
    and in shame,
And his voice was no river, it was the small sweetness after a long briar
    is plucked from under a nail.
I would not pull him back through the scratch and laceration of the needle,
    his yodel swaying now like the imperfect pirouette of a skater.
The engines are gone that towed his boxcars out of the coalfields.

Refashioned as a mall, the station catches in a dull web of suspended tracks,
  and Rodgers is no ghost
To guide me through side alleys of poolhalls and pawnshops, to stand
  with me on State Street,
Both of us loathing the city's sandblasted bricks, the newly installed dogwoods
That are blossoming already in their tended circles of salt-treated boards.

Most of my country abhors filth and denounces a ruin, but I want that heart
  that ripens in desolation,
Not the showy glass of cathedrals but the bent poles under a sagging awning.
I stand across from the drygoods and the jewelry stores, dreaming of brothels,
And I wait awhile on the wrought-iron bench in front of the smashed saloon
  where the heavy matriarchs went hushing the fiddles.
A ghost loves a low place where the street sinks through a broken drain
  and finds in a pool of oil
Under a rusting Cadillac the last ripple in the long-lingering odor of horses.
Daily, he assumes the untunable shape. He escapes the longing
  for perfection.
If I must sing at all of renewal, let me gather a choir from all the losses.
  I will laugh again with
The left-handed spirits. I will dance in this sacred alley of the Protestants.

Coming down Sand Mountain, many things moved with me in the car,
   cosmic aphasia after a spat,
A staticky Jonathan Winters tape, the *Best of the Rolling Stones*,
And then I saw them, hatless, ungoverned, decamping from the church,
   a thread that flared to rope
And sprawled across the parking lot and knotted under trees:
   the bald and freshly permed,
Many with dark coats and red ties or matching purses and shoes,
Innocuous farmers with their retinues of fledgling weightlifters,
   maiden aunts of philosophy students,
Ex-coaches of insurance salesmen and guidance counselors,
Architects plotting the aesthetics of Alabama Savings & Loans,
   great flocculent femmes fatales
Trailing the mountainous sexual wonder of sixteen-year-old boys.

Walt Whitman, snow-jobber and cataloguer of American dreams,
   demographer of miracles,
There was just that instant there, I boiled them in one glimpse
   and thought they'd maybe caucused
For a wedding or a death, or did they love the Lord so much
   they'd come
On Sunday, Wednesday, and now again on Friday afternoon?
   And some of these, too,
I guessed, had formed the mob I'd seen Saturday two weeks before
   that looked so magisterial, stentorian, Greek,
As it uncoiled in a stark festoon of white sheets and dunce's peaks
   toward some vitriolic
Welder's speech against Earl Warren, Satan, the communists,
   the niggers, and the Jews:
Distinguish them singly or mark them in the curve where they
   began to blur
And fade along the piedmont of fescue, anguses, and machines.

Were these the faces you cheered westward, and numinous bodies,
    yet unpublished in the secret pages of the grass,
Or does the flying vision always fracture on closer inspection
    of a part?
Another mile of farms, the mountains sank to hills, a sorghum
    mill, a spotted mule
And then, emblazoned on a barn, a painting of a waterfall
    where, later, I would stop
And grip the rail and watch the violent, white, transfiguring
    stalk of water
That seemed to rear as it drove down and shattered on the rocks
    and clarified beyond
In many little streams that muddled on and vanished in the trees
    in just that way,
I thought, that death might settle into things, and still, father
    of joy and understanding, I didn't leap.
I stood there glowing under the patient faces of the leaves.

It is good, after all, to pause and lick one's genitalia,
To hunch one's shoulders and gag, regurgitating lunch,
To mark one's curb and grass, to bay when the future beckons
    from the nose,
Not to exhaust so much of the present staring into the flat face
    of a machine,
Not to spend so much of the logic and the voice articulating a complex
    whimper of submission,
But to run with a full stomach under the sun, to play in the simple water
    and to wallow oneself dry in the leaves,
To take the teeth in the neck, if it comes to that,
If it comes to little and lean and silent, to take the position of the stone,
    even to hide under the stone,
But not to ride up the spine of the building with the acid scalding
    the gut,
Not to sit at a long table, wondering
How not to howl when the tall one again personifies the organization,
Speaking of the customs in remote precincts and the manufacture
    of weapons there
Or the near Edens where the pitted balls fly over the tonsured lawns.

Dear mammals, help me, the argument with flesh is too fierce
    if it outrides time
And shocks numb the stubborn, beautiful muscles of the heart.
See, in the memorial gardens, how even the cry struggles in its trap
    under that black hat like a flower.
In the long rows of tombstones, the ones who were eaten betray nothing
    of the fear that brought them.
And it was their silence that marked them, day after oathless day,
    until they were covered by the silent lawns.
Better to take the mud in the hands and holler for no reason,
    to praise the strange

Alchemy of mud and rain: there is sex; there is food.
It is good to say anything in the spirit of hair and breasts
  and warm blood,
And not to deny the private knowledge, not to wonder how
  not to speak of death,
And not to deny the knowledge of death, not to invent the silence,
Not to wonder how not to say the words of love.

Its huge numbers include us, our cars, houses, and substantial goods,
    but the numbers
Do not stop north of Lake George or south of the Rio Grande.
There is a large number that stands for the Atlantic.
There is a very large number that stands for the Pacific.
Last winter a number of Mexicans smuggling their muscles north
    in a shut railway car
Suffocated and was added to a larger number, which includes
    the teenage pregnancy and whooping crane,
And will it be enough, when the great condor and sea tortoise
    have shrunken to one,
To weigh the hour of ovulation against the bounty of the sperm?

It is not just the children to come. Also, the rat, the opossum,
    the raccoon, and the mourning dove
Have traveled the sewer main and, dead, mounted sufficient work
To be counted among the problems, which include the Mexicans,
    the Ethiopians, and acid rain.
Our problems are so numerous, it is very essential that we count
The boats, their size and type, and the numbers of life preservers,
    fire extinguishers, and horns.
And it must be clear, even to the forgotten and almost extinct Arapaho,
Why one of us must keep the books of the crows and the ledgers
    of the bees,
And, glumly, another counts the instruments after the failed operation
    as the final
Number is wired to the big toe, and the hands are crossed neatly.

Otherwise, the dark vector keeps on rising on that unlined graph,
    and we feel,
From far south, across the plunging of that gulf, in cities
    uncharmable and vast,
Those streets where a number of the just deceased are left to rot—
There is no telling when the government trucks will come
    and pick up a token number,

No reckoning how many each of the deceased has disappointed,
How many children, crippled, clever, gifted, how many cooperative
    and uncooperative sexual partners.
The unnumbered fruits rot, unprofitable, shameful;
The coat of paint is left to peel, no command is given to recover it,
    and there is nothing to say
After the mortar attack, when the reporters go like maggots,
    working the torn nests.

Or if there is a story, say it was too much to say even a single
    palm tree, the shade of the mission
Where the old one-legged man cut tires into sandals,
Or those bluest of lakes cupped in the craters of dead volcanoes.
Say there were too many saints and holidays, too many small people
Following donkeys up roads that vanished into gullies and trees,
    too many siestas.
Say the mathematicians left, the multiplications were so various,
    and there was nothing left to divide.

But record these zeros, ripening on vines beyond the infected wells,
    look carefully
At the mountain devoid of trees, the men passed out on the streets,
And the women bending to irritate their stony rows of corn,
    for something
Like history is trying to take place in secret meetings and bombs,
Something that does not include us, though we are there in force,
    counting the dead,
And the aid we read of sending underwrites the new resorts
    we will visit perhaps,
When the sense of history is strongest, just after the peace is signed.

COUNTING POTATOES

And with one booted stroke his pitchfork brought
Them plopping up from the fresh blossom of loam
Like the heads of children shaved for surgery
Or bald statesmen—this one Khrushchev, that one Ike—
And *Jesus Christ* and *Son-of-a-bitch* he went
As he went at a steady clip, vanished over the ridge
And reappeared, collecting heads in a gunnysack,
While I played mason up the clod walls of my fort,
Waiting to tally the bushels he could not count.
Colorless and abstract hulls, what did I know
Of mindless work or hangovers or bitter sons—
The erudition of that sensitive, ignorant man?
By noon, he'd stoop in dirt and scratch a clock,
But the shadows have circled back to empty fields:
Gray days in early November, cool mornings
Of thirty years later, when I think of it all,
How slowly the moon must have passed over the valley
More than ten thousand times, and how quickly,
When he died and there was no soul left to save,
The congregation fell to squabbling over some
Verse a sleepy abbot mistranslated from the Greek
Nearly fifteen hundred years ago, but no one alive
Remembered the cry or face buried in each word
That curses and blesses the ground and insists
There is nothing, and nothing is not nothing,
But if there is something else, a farther interior, unknown
And delicate, clutched in the body's violent wish
To emerge from the ordinary mist and stand unstinting
In a higher place, let it be from that earthiest flesh,
That root and core, that potato, that I compose a faith.

THE PRIVILEGE

That I took the kickoff, feinted, spun twice, sidestepped a tackle,
  and, glorified,
Ran fifty-five yards in the open field before the safety sheared me
  at the knees and I rolled
Down a gully under a barbwire fence and looked up into the sullen,
  algebraic face of a cow;
But, also, that I came from the dermatologist with my brow parched
  by sun lamps and dry ice
And walked the logging road up Cooper Mountain and spoke to trees;
  that my mute hysteria
On bridges, escalators, and telephones ripened gradually into fear;
  that age did not dignify me;
Also, that I risked my fourth year meditating and erecting cities
  under the old house
And stayed there with the rotting wine cask and the brown bottles
  until my head
Bumped against the floor joists and the bus shunted me off to school;
  not just that my long immersion
In ink filled me with visions of invisibility and supernatural powers;
Not just that I addled years, dividing and subtracting, spelling
  the words I already knew;
But, also, that the shy philosopher I plucked from a party in Tuscaloosa
  and squired to New Orleans
Broke down in Pat O'Brien's and I waited for her in the bleached hall
  of the charity ward
And watched the red-haired intern cover the dead indigent with a sheet
  and suffered
His lecture on the epistemological and literary virtues of Ayn Rand;
  that the night
I lugged her through the foggy streets and left her with the Jesuit priest
  still has some truck with me
When I strap my son into the car or push him past the gleaming lawns;
  that it stands with the nights
Of mescaline, the nights of abortions, and the nights of betrayals;
  nothing will shake it

From the totem of my forty-second year, even if I arrive at clarity,
    with some bitter water for the lilies
With some sweet nitrogen for the willows, for that was the privilege,
    to carry the light itself
And not burn down, not yet, and I will not turn Judas to the madness.

I still don't know why the purple leotard and orange mohawk of the giant
    punker rattling up onto the Kensington bus
Pricked more than thrilled me, or why the natty, atavistic, beet-
    and-celery-plaid blazer
Slung across the back of a drunk panhandling through Union Station
Made me wish him blind and musical more than rich and lucid,
But I believe that my cousin Alice, when Joey died, came to the funeral
    parlor in faded jeans
And a T-shirt out of respect, brandished that simple ensemble of cottons
    like the flag of a defeated country,
And when my Uncle Limuel, her father, saw her, it hit him like a tax
    levied on all of propriety.
His face darkened. His jaw flinched. I don't know what he said to her,
    or she to him,
As they drove the backroads home, or while she changed in the bathroom,
But she returned in the black dress and white blouse of regulation sorrow.

As for the service then, it dragged: stupid and sad medley of sentimentia,
    stolen aphorisms, and off-key duets,
When maybe the Flying Lizards should have jammed on "Stairway to
    Heaven," for a few of Joey's bunch,
A collar-scruff of small-town freaks and homosexuals, slunk at the fringe
    in chains and leather shirts.
I don't know why else my aunt let the Peck brothers lay out Joey,
    tieless, in a stenciled denim jacket,
Like a runaway napping in a mall or a country singer sleeping off a buzz.
Because grief hides an inner violence, it requires a march and uniforms,
    but I know, too,
How, earlier, just after the wreck and the implausible, cryptic surgery,
    the mortician
Took the blond hair from an envelope and, lock by lock, fashioned
    the exact contour
To set off the face he had so patiently reconstructed with putty and wax,
    as though that smile, marooned
Between awe and bemusement, would wire a cosmic message from the grass,

And that join with a subtler thing, a signal look that flows in everydayness,
    perhaps unifying us, but also
Sundering and balkanizing us into tribes, also forming a hedge and a wall,
    beyond which
The modes of taste and sexual orientation, the ideologies, creeds, and styles
Ease us from the showroom new and drive us awhile and leave us for scrap
    out on some hill
That overlooks a homestead our ancestors hacked and gutted from the plain,
    which was like the place I stood
When the compressor hissed and Joey sank like a piston in its dark block.
But what I meant to get to earlier, before the service, and the silly, moot
    contention over black and blue,
Was the rage I lived out each day, wanting to fit in, but also to stand off,
    not just from that place,
But that whole year with its polyester leisure suits catching like Edsels
    in the nation's throat
And the great surfeit of the mills curling into lapels, cuffs, and pleats.

Blues that persist in grays, I see the age, Nixon fallen, the war ending,
    the schools desegregated,
The suits I had to wear to get jobs—even the bad ones, roofing houses
    or loading and unloading trucks—
And the jeans I favored, patched at the crotch and knees, the Turkish
    caftans and faintly urinous Indian sandals,
Which seemed then to connect by some oblique cultural umbilicus to Free
    Love and Peace,
Those movements consuming the last arc of their cycle, shining like dew
    and burning away,
Unraveling threads, the dashikis and hippie caps, packed away in boxes,
The boxes of beads and capes, the boxes of flowered shirts and sheets—
    thrown on the dump
Or consigned to the thrift shops, but faded now and somehow drab—
The bell-bottom pants and tie-dyed shirts we touch and draw back from,
    as though it were those
Clothes and not the skin we bury deep and wouldn't be caught dead in.

DIPLOMACY

Now that she was gone and the two daughters had agreed
Not to bury her in the pearls, here were the pearls,
The single string laid out across the center of the bed

Like teeth that one and then the other paused to touch,
But briefly, what with renters coming soon, and much
Still to divvy up: a spinning wheel with one cracked

Spoke, a dirty Chinese rug, and other, heavier stuff—
Enormous desks and chests-of-drawers I'd have to lug
By turns to each truck and load, and then unload

And load again should one, perhaps reliving some ancient
Childhood slight, reclaim a gift she'd given long ago,
Though this was not just greed, but greed distilled

In grief and dripping prose: "Remember," the younger
Would say, and lift a decades-out-of-fashion gown:
"Dawn's wedding, that garden party. Well, take it now;

It fairly swallows me," and then, after a while, mildly:
"Myra says she always favored me but liked you best."
And who would not, I thought but did not say. Both

Were good, and generous enough, returning often to sit
With her all through the weeks she suffered, and later,
In those bleaker, uglier months when there was nothing

But the gesture, no hope but that she'd die, and soon.
Both had that look, Scotch-Irish, fiery, resolute,
Though the older was poorer, shabbier, dressed in a thin

Green work shirt and pedal pushers that kept slipping
Down to reveal the welting left by the elastic band,
So you got the sense that not just this but her whole life

Had gone sour, the way, with such a grim and martyr-
Like display of charity, she'd grant the younger one,
Who was dark and pretty, a chipped dish or fraying coat,

And then, when the younger had taken it in both hands,
Fingered it indifferently, and placed it, with much
Show of stealth, in the Goodwill box, she'd snatch

It back and, for an instant, turn, not mean exactly,
But predatory, her eyes scanning the archipelagoes
Of castoff shoes and clothes, the pressure building up

Until you knew she'd say something, not much, a dig
Perhaps, a minor thorn, but enough so you knew then,
Not just the pearls, which she would finally take

From the bed and hang gently around her sister's neck,
But everything she'd lose — she'd list it all, but later,
Once the sister had gone. She'd grieve. All afternoon

She'd kneel, and as she scrubbed, she'd add it up:
The slow work, the power in the dirt, and the living
Fabric dragging on her shoulders like a worn suit.

"Lizards," he'd say, dispensing with local men, and then resheath his pen
    and huff back to his drafting table,
A fiber board pristined with vinyl and overhung with the ambiguous,
    linked appendages of maybe a dozen modular lights,
One of which, now, by some unfathomable kink of logic, he'd bring
    screeching down above
His latest renderings of nunlike, mestiza hens I'd named like missiles:
    the Star 5000, the T-100 Egg Machine.

Those days of fruitless scratching on a pad, those nights of Klee and Rilke,
    and what abortifacient labor
Leaves, instead of money, that sense of energy troweled out and slapped up,
    no more than a phrase or two
That sticks, a sketch, no novel, no painting, only time whining irrevocably
    and the feeling
Of events put off or missed: openings, autograph parties—What else?

The grudging knowledge that, even in this, we were lucky: recession
    was on; Vietnam still shipped its dead.
I had the job because a friend knew a friend; he was someone's son:
    a cardiologist or an architect—I never learned.
Except for the boss, Devon, a transplanted Englishman with waxed mustache
    who chain-smoked Virginia Slims and despised Americans,
And Gwendolyn, his Phi Beta Kappa secretary, we worked alone in a kind
    of paneled coop they'd rigged

Above a shop that printed invitations and sold used office machines,
    or we'd go out as a team—
Cullman, Springdale, Gainesville—on this particular morning on a road
    just dusted with the season's first snow,
Stravinsky on the stereo, the piney Georgia hills, our usual patter, high
    culture, high art,
And then the building, massive, white, impregnable, our destination then,
    where we'd come to make something,

One of those brochures or tracts that aspire, through much lyrical glut
    and bedazzlement of facts,
To be taken as an article, objective, empirical: four thousand *bons mots*
    of cant replete with scale drawings
And headed "The World's First Totally Integrated Poultry Processing Plant."
    Was that art? Is this?
Embellished in four colors, translated into Dutch, Spanish, and Portuguese?
    That moment when he said it, "Lizards"?

Or later, when the door opened and the stench of bowels, lungs, and hearts
    welled up to us from the line
That we could just now make out through the steam, that first denuded
    glimpse of carcasses shedding slaughter
And strung by the talons as they moved through the faceless maze of women
    as in some gothic laundry
Fellini might have drudged up for the illuminati in heartfelt homage
    to the enduring spirit of Soutine.

Just that moment then, before a big man, someone officious, a plant
    manager or engineer, herded us in,
A handshake, a nod, and saying, "Here, take these," he gave us each a bag
    marked "Sanitation Suit,"
The silly bag-boy hats, paper coats, and thin latex gloves that now we
    had to haul on as he led us
Through the machines—the stunner, the killer, the plucker, the eviscerator,
    the de-lunger, the stripper, the chiller—

Each with its grisly attendant, those women, those Picassoesque smocks
    be-spattered with yellow and red,
That proletariat chorus line, winking, emoting cool or hard-to-get,
    pregnant high school dropouts,
Tattooed grandmothers, chubby peroxide blondes wagging their fannies
    for the wheels.
So I knew, before the word had formed in the brain, before my friend had
    covered his lips with one hand,

And said it in that whisper that frames the sneer and gives it a secret
      eloquence, that it was coming,
Like one drop melting from a high icicle, falling, and spitting against a rock,
      "Lizards"—
And then, though how could any have heard, those women, as though
      in antiphony—what is the word?—words?—
"Sang," "jeered," "hooted," "whistled," "booed," "crowed," "honked,"
      "squawked"?

If you had ever heard five hundred North Georgia women in full-throated
      glory, parodying the morning cacophony of a barnyard
And knew that sound was meant for you, you would know how God
      sometimes
Will call a brother out of the terrible fields, and why the rest of that day
      stands out on the map of days,
Even the Chicken Teriyaki they served at lunch, and the ride back, snow
      skunking the ridges—our big idea

To name one bird and follow it from the chicken house through the plant,
      but gently, describing the genius
Of each machine, and on to the grocery store, where, yes, that was it,
      a young housewife, no, a widow would pick it up,
Bells would ring, a handsome man, the president of the company, we'd say,
      would step out from behind the frozen dinners,
And present a check, ten thousand dollars, and then—dissolve to dinner—
      an idea of tenderness, we'd call it,

But would it fly? Each day, I'd write, he'd draw. "Lizards," he'd say
      by way of greeting and goodbye.
Each night at the strip-bar in the shopping center, we'd drink on it. "Rilke
      is greater than Keats."
"Warhol follows naturally from Mondrian, but what I'm after in my work—
      call it Caravaggio with a gun—
Is riskier, everything exposed between the observation and display"; then,
      "Imagine what it means,

Living in a place like this, loving men — Men? — Reptiles, lizards, slopes!" —
We'd see them crawling from the bathroom to the stools, and then the
  women would mount them,
Shut their eyes, and grind down hard in that mockery of a dance they do
    that seems at first
A quote of love's best motions, then just work, then the promise withdrawn,
  gone, the money and the girl —

Some guys would shrug and grin; others bluster up, throats tightening, fists
  purpling above the watered gin,
Before the rage guttered in an epithet or joke they'd still be slurring
  as they stumbled out into the cold.
Some nights we'd stay until the place grew quiet, late, and later, a fierce
  clinking of bottles; now light
Above the steel mills; now voices: dogs, birds. What would become of us?

THE LIFE I DID NOT LIVE

It is happening out there, I see it coming
And turn, it is trailing a woman I knew
And kids who briefly, oddly, resemble me,
Before it vanishes among those streets
I never took and vows I could not keep,
Like bubbles that leap from the aquarium's
Tended dunes and blink above the fish,
And still I feel it wallow at the verge
Of everything I saw but could not feel.
I see the honest lawyer I wanted to be
And the archaeologist I might have been;
And others, too, the junkie, the thief,
The patient addict of adrenaline and fear,
Stillborn in my twenties, when I stood
Transfixed at the meridian of gifts
And chose by choosing not to choose.
But I am forty. I feel the stratifying
Coals of old ambitions oxidize to ash.
One life to hold, one night that weeps
From the block of all the time there is:
My son, the center of attention, looms
Like Genghis Khan above his Lincoln Logs
To flush the ghosts from the living room,
And, shrinking into sleep, hears the water
Thrum against the faucet's aging grip.
The noise of every other life subsides,
Far off, tranquilizing whine of gears,
And then one drip that brings an ocean
Of questions brimming on the mute lip:
Was I happy? Did I do what I wished?
Knots pop from the tightness of beams,
And moonlight gilds the lawns with promise.
By midnight each tamed spirit will
Start up howling and groveling at its leash.

MEDITATION AT HOME

Sampling country in the margin between subdivisions,
We had not settled in the hush beyond the last houses
When a doe and two fawns leapt up and bolted south

Toward the national forest beyond the Chautauqua Road,
And because we froze, the landscape froze in our eyes.
We heard the water tick between the moss and stone.

Then the three Schwinns loomed up from the deer's bed.
Void of wheels and gears, they seemed to haunt the weeds,
And though we knew the thieves who hid them there

Were not dangerous men but tribes of neighborhood boys,
When I lifted one of the frames and saw the ants cascade
From the rusted sprocket, I felt some promise breached—

Like the bounty of our old farm, its decades-fallow fields
Spilling a two-hundred-acre yard behind the rotted barn—
And then the city embodied in those ants rushing my arm,

The many places that were the land, granted and bound.
Wordsworth thought of setting as thought, seedling hopes,
Everglades of ideologies pollinating whenever he walked,

So we walked the kept wilderness back to our front door,
So Sunday's violence played out far away on artificial turf,
But the players moving on screen seemed kin to grass

And those animals who slept among the stripped machines.
Six months later and that tract has been profitably sold,
The meadow bulldozed. This is the first day of survey stakes

And thirty-three red flags, each representative of a home,
A family, a dog who may stray far enough to startle deer,
To invoke the rancor of skunks or the arrows of porcupines,

And, today, for the first time, I thought of leaving America.
Enraged by its suburban heaths and seaside condominiums,
Its rivers graying in the drums of washing machines,

Its frontiers shrunken where frogs perch on fountain lips
Or the heretical flamingo drips rust onto the sacred lawn,
I stamped in the subsoil where the road would continue,

And measured the distance between feathers and iron,
And cooled then, and having nowhere better to go, turned
And walked back down the pavement to what space I owned.

To come here on a Sunday
And find the long asphalt
Ribbon through the woods
Unoccupied, to follow
The mossy steps cut down
The face of the rock, to
Walk all day and not fall,
To find no meaning, neither
In the lily of the valley
Nor the seeds of berries
Shining in ambiguous scat,
And not to look for meaning,
Not to long for the name
Of the god, but to move silently,
Steadily along the cobbles
Of the dried creek, to climb
And descend, stepping over
Deadfall, a woman and a man,
There was nothing else,
The great store
Of the peopled world closed,
Uncomplicated midsummer
Before us like a plain, time
Of thoughtlessness, time
Of labor beside the road,
Time of deerfly, flea season
After rain when the rock
Is cool and all our longing
Some wet-nursery under a cliff,
Some woods pool we wade
For our fattening hearts,
For the lost soul of the
Nineteenth century, just walking
Then, saying nothing of this.

ARGUMENT OVER A PLASTIC CHAIR

When I thought of nature, I saw fescue lifting the old road,
Tearing at the shoulders, spidering the black lace of ruin;
Saw acorns, like jackhammers, blasting from underneath,

Saw even the mimosa, that cottony tree, cracking the seal,
Imposing the seed's buried software of blossom and bough.
City, forest, and sky: I could not see the whole of it.

No lines were there. Not where moles burrowed into steel.
Not where sidewalks stopped and maples began like weekends.
Still, I can see the chair as she saw it, not formed but made.

She comes from Kingsport, where the forest hides deep
Under the boulevards, where the big diesels pound all night
Past Eastman's three thousand acres of industrial tanks

That look gutted and bare as the tubes of a junked radio.
She sees the lights of new houses clouding the thickets,
Sees Olin's spilt mercury shiver against the spines of trout

And eats no sugar for her child, but spoons of beneficent grain,
Roughage for the bowels, peas and garlic for the fetal heart.
The argument did not start with the chair, only she took

Herself for science, me for art. She marked my clutter
Against her order. I saw my poems ramble against her charts.
The chair was just there, hard by the wall. It was stark

And institutional, dyed oranger than any simple orange
Of sunrise or leaves. I'd say it was our nature to sit down,
To push words or oil toward plastic that would not rot.

That we had no side apart from trees that would be oil,
Oil that would be chairs. That even our ideas came up
Like ferns and took shape out of the humus of desire.

She'd take the other side, say we stood apart from plants
With ruin and otherworldly chairs. She'd mention plutonium,
Its long half-life, though this I'd claim for nature, too—

What was the use? She'd see, ahead, each moot point
I'd make about the world go black while her child turned
In the clutter of all we'd made that would not go back.

THE PRIVACY OF WOMEN

Of course it's a power no man could withstand, all that
        forbidding aura
Of the glance and the long sweetness of the slow analysis,
Sweetness that drew him
                                into the muscle of the fruit,
That sent him away
                        who had given away the flint prod
Of his fire
            and stood moon-open in the open spaces,
No god but that sweetness and the paralysis before daybreak
In the eons before love,
                        even the stone knife caught
In that mystique of flesh, that dense charisma of the blood.

                                *

Tenderness of the bison
                        twitching its fly-bespotted flank,
Certain green, certain grove, and what came before the words,
        the wrenching of hunger
Or birth, unmerciful, certain as the rock in its arrival,
Pure sweetness of the berry
                                to which he returned and returned,
Before the promise that took the dark shape of the berry.

                                *

She glossed me young, made heartstroke of namesound, combing
        out her black hair,
Left homemade jelly in those old jars
                                you see now in shops,
Shaped flour and lard,
                        the simple shape of my longing,
Praised God, praised music, gentled, in lightning and thunder,
The terrified mare,
                grandmother, salt stoic, named for a flower,

I touched each dress, each coat, the closet void now of her hands,
    the black rubber boots
She had worn to the lot and returned in, gloved in dung,
    empty and shining.

*

And she loved the clean undershine of fine cabinets, chairbacks
    grooved and carved
With the rising and falling arcs of the shapes of flowers,
The minor key
        of her sad song, to which we turned, returning
To the common argument over everything, which was larger
    than the sweetness,
But transcended and augmented by sweetness.

*

When we have touched many breasts, we think we know the earth
That loves us,
        but the argument clings to the lovemaking,
The argument over everything holds us glistening in its vice,
And when the breasts are withdrawn, we are the shadows
Of the breasts,
        as the wife is the shadow of the mother,
The dark, rich seawater, the swamp, and the forty-foot loam
    of the midwestern plains
Will roll over us
        as certainly as we walk down the avenue
And imagine in high windows some distant evolution of pines.

*

I have to go back to the first things
          circled around the fire,
Ancient petition
        when the hunt returned, grateful for the corn,
Woman and man dividing everything,
            sun, stars, and moon,

Both the necessary and the mistaken decisions
                              to move on,
The chart in the womb, the chart in the testicles, the treasure map
Where I am marked
                    in the living hieroglyphics of the genes
And feel myself drawn and quartered by desire's own knife.

                                      *

All things shining,
                    even our public and glittering grief,
A gift,
        and the underthings of the beloved, the regal stain
Of dark berries,
                  but the lovesong and the song of her loss,
I can no longer name them,
                            I have forgotten how they were made,
As though she had vanished through the eye of the needle
      that sews
The rot into vegetation and slipped the unfolding of my brain.

                                      *

The age of men has passed,
                            genocidal whims of the masculine science,
Dominion of all loveliness,
                            green words from the back of the class,
And now turning away from the lives of men,
                                    I was not one of those
Who clustered on the easy girls
                          outside the Pickwick and the Mill,
Not all the time stuck in the sweetness.
                              So much of the prose of duty
Has us scrawled in the margins: slow nights at the shipping docks,
I thought of Lawrence,
                  his star-crossed, improbable, symbolic lovers —

They are not our story,
                    who burn briefly in that moment
That is shipwreck and rescue.
                              I was not chosen for any loveliness
But chose loveliness.

                              *

Chose as any young man would choose
                              what he thought would endure
The lie of gentleness
                    when she lay in that red welt of time,
Stretched inside out
                    on the interminable desert day of birthing,
And spoke Samuel, our one son, I had no more empathy to learn,
But stood in the blinding room
                              of that hospital blasted by snow,
And could not speak or cut the cord
                              when the scissors were offered,
But was as one who feeds the queen the sticky muscle of the blossom
And went from there
                    to give some comfort to my daughter.

                              *

For many who loved me have mired in their names and old faces,
And are lost to me,
                    for I have forsaken their knowledge
And company for this home, far away on a remote shelf of time,
I cannot reach them.
                    My brother, who taught me four cities
And the singing shapes of vowels, is a stranger to me.
                                        His poems
Are scrawled on napkins and the backs of paper bags, his ashes
Are scattered across the gardens of two beer halls.

                              *

He stands at the beginning of my mind, but I did not keep him
From his life,
                        strung on the cleats of the winter rain,
Who had no real harbor
                                but the iron bed of a dump truck
And cried in his sleep,
                                for he dreamed of his dead mother
Resurrected in the flesh of a bride,
                                        but I had my own bride,
My own daughter to carry over the mud and broken bottles.

                                *

It does not say in any book that the division will be clean
Between mother and son
                        or father and daughter
Who would remain tactful in the glue of the unyielding bond
Even as they are swept out in the drift of strangeness
Until one stands alone
                        with the dirt that starts memory
On the salt road to legend by gilt enlargements and routine omissions
Until the strangeness is made presentable,
                                        and the other
Slowly begins to take place in the stock memorabilia
That will be as a funnel to the focus on ordinary things
That were trusted and shined,
                                and now given over to strangers.

                                *

My love, my mother, my one daughter, my song, my salt evocation,
Given completely to their keeping,
                                I give up my last shyness
As my grandfather was undressed and lowered into the water
Of his last bath
                and the nurse unrolled the pink scroll
Of his shrunken genitals,
                                and from the sweetness of her nature,

Cleaned the crusted glans and prepared him for the last bed,
So my wife has known me
                              in my sloth and my drunkenness,
In the tears that were not for her,
                              but the forsaken life
She could not know,
                              for she had led me from far to this house
And could not know back there
                              one of the dead from another.

                              *

So I approach my mother from the alley of my long grief
To tell her of this birth
                              this month of her mother's death
And sit at the plain table
                              borne up on irrepressible
Waves of pleasure and loss,
                              with the one voice of family
Tightening around me like wooden cartilage aching in an old ship,
But she goes back to fixing,
                              she turns from her final
Knowledge of the dark
                              to the dead god of her mother,
And will not tell me, but goes back to bringing in
And carrying out,
                              she scrubs the counters to a fine shine,
Long she admirals dust into pans, long the waters run.

                              *

Only late at night, there is laughter in the living room.
There are secrets opening
                              in stories of the dead
Who resemble so much our sleeping daughters and sons.
Surely there is a mystery inside the rising and setting sun,
Surely there is an ocean
                              inside the star she wished upon

That hip-splaying children
                        should crest on that slow-
Bursting fountain and suffer the miracle-anointing gust
Of ordinary light,
                        whose lives become our lives drifting
Away from her
                        and drawn out in the cascade of diasporas
Until we return by new roads
                        as many have come earlier
Bearing the bag of old guilts
                        to the address of sorrow
With one greeting: *The ballast of death is love.*

I glimpsed you just as I was dying, cluster of grapes
Dipping toward the clear river, startled white birds,
Wisest and wildest and loveliest who lay with me
All those years while flesh opened like a door
And the old poignant steam of creation rose
Above the calibrated hours of numbing appointments
As when the odors of coffee and croissants briefly
Ascend the carnal spices of the delicatessen,
And the throat hurts for the beauty of one night,
Which will not last; even as the feeling begins
It is gone into the morning's etherizing rind.
A blind music holds the brain down to its joy,
The hand plunging or the cheek glowing with blood,
Consumption, sexual and mortal, in which we flare,
Blue as fuses at the silent core of the trance,
And the world of scorned treasures burns back:
A boot, a shredded Goodyear tire, the Atlantic
Behind you that same evening a dead porpoise
And Russian detergent bottle washed ashore.
You were wearing your blue jeans and white shirt.
Small bones curdled of starlight, salt privacy
Of elbows and knees, secret estuary of skin,
Your hair was combed back from your face
And hung in a straight ponytail down your back.
It was the first year, I think, that you thought
Not to put red on the lips, black around the eyes.
Hands with short nails, voice of plain speech,
Bringing on the final exorcisms of courtship,
I noticed you among the actual stars—illicit,
Undeniable, intolerable, but grounding all this
Ten-year unwarrantied life. I have said next
To nothing, plumber of dark gray drains,
Resuscitator of dead stoves. It was never
As though breasts would rebuild Dresden

Or thighs resurrect the ride up San Juan Hill.
It was never as though you thought of me
As a train weapon or car. To speak of love
Is to speak of knowing, but stand oblivion
On its end; let me be that ocean, dark
And unlettered and arriving only at itself,
Though I keep you in mind, the flesh bond
And public secret, our dumb beauty in the best hours.

NOTES AND ACKNOWLEDGMENTS

Lama, which appears in "Fun in El Salvador," is a cryptogamous plant that proliferates in dense layers in the volcanic crater lakes of Central America.

Grateful acknowledgment is made to the following journals, in which some of these poems were first published, many in earlier versions: *The American Poetry Review*: "At the Miracle Mall," "Fantasia of the Bride," "On the Eleventh Anniversary of Divorce"; *Chelsea*: "Diplomacy," "Failed Memory Exercise," "The Privilege"; *Cutbank*: "At Summerford's Nursing Home," "Moment of Whitman"; *Denver Quarterly*: "Hollywood"; *Grand Street*: "Shame the Monsters"; *The Indiana Review*: "Enough"; *The Kenyon Review*: "Born Again," "Ecology of Heaven," "Meditation at Home," "Romance of the Poor"; *Michigan Quarterly Review*: "Contempt"; *The New England Review*: "Apocalyptic Narrative," "Grand Projection," "Second Nature," "Speaking Up," "Thirty-one Flavors of Houses"; *The New Virginia Review*: "Argument over a Plastic Chair," "Progress Alley"; *The Paris Review*: "The Privacy of Women"; *Pequod*: "Threads"; *The Southern Review*: "A Story of the South Pacific," "The Bridge," "White Mexicans."

"The Bridge" was republished in *Ars Poetica*; "Grand Projection" was republished in *The Best American Poetry 1993* (Louise Gluck, guest editor); "Progress Alley" and "Romance of the Poor" were republished in *Walk on the Wild Side: Contemporary Urban American Poetry*.

Thanks to Southern Illinois University–Carbondale for release time, which allowed me to finish this book, and to Gloria Jones, Carlos Nixon, Borden Plunkett, Katya Rice, Hans Rudnick, Sherod Santos, Margot Schilpp, Dave Smith, and Jack Vespa for specific suggestions on poems. I also would like to thank David Baker, James Dickey, Tom Disch, Jorie Graham, Donald Hall, Kent Haruf, Terry Hummer, David Lehman, Richard Peterson, Richard Russo, Jean Stein, and James Whitehead for their support and encouragement, and to express special thanks to my editor, Peter Davison, for his uncompromising criticism of earlier versions of this manuscript.